Desert Skin

DESERT

Thomas Miller

The University of Utah Press   *Salt Lake City*

Essay by Edward Abbey

Library of Congress Cataloging-in-Publication Data
Miller, Thomas, 1943–
      Desert skin / Thomas Miller ; essay by Edward Abbey.
         p.   cm.
      ISBN 0-87480-460-4
      1. Landscape photography—Colorado Plateau.   2. Aerial
photography—Colorado Plateau.   3. Deserts—Colorado Plateau—
Pictorial works.   I. Abbey, Edward, 1927–   .   II. Title.
TR660.5.M54   1994
779'.367913'092—dc20
                                                            94-19293

To Brant and Marsha
for lending wings of different color

Contents

Come On In

he canyon country of southern Utah and northern Arizona—the Colorado Plateau— is something special. Something strange, marvelous, full of wonders. As far as I know there is no other region on earth much like it, or even remotely like it. Nowhere else have we had this lucky combination of vast sedimentary rock formations exposed to a desert climate, a great plateau carved by major rivers—the Green, the San Juan, the Colorado— into such a surreal land of form and color. Add a few volcanoes, the standing necks of which can still be seen, and cinder cones and lava flows, and at least four separate laccolithic mountain ranges nicely distributed about the region, and more hills, holes, humps and hollows, reefs, folds, salt domes, swells and grabens, buttes, benches and mesas, synclines, monoclines, and anticlines than you can ever hope to see and explore in one lifetime, and you begin to arrive at an approximate picture of the plateau's surface appearance.

An approximate beginning. A picture framed by sky and time in the world of natural appearances. Despite the best efforts of a small army of writers, painters, photographers, scientists, explorers, Indians, cowboys, and wilderness guides, the landscape of the Colorado Plateau lies still beyond the reach of reasonable words. Or unreasonable representation. This is a landscape that has to be seen to be believed, and even then, confronted directly by the senses, it strains credulity.

Comprehensible, yes. Perhaps nowhere is the basic structure of the earth's surface so clearly, because so nakedly, revealed. And yet—when all we know about it is said and measured and tabulated, there remains something in the soul of the place, the spirit of the whole, that cannot be fully assimilated by the human imagination.

My terminology is far from exact; certainly not scientific. Words like "soul" and "spirit" make vague substitutes for a hard effort toward understanding. But I can offer no better. The land here is like a great book or a great symphony; it invites approaches toward comprehension on many levels, from all directions.

The geologic approach is certainly primary and fundamental, underlying the attitude and outlook that best support all others, including the insights of poetry and the wisdom of religion. Just as the earth itself forms the indispensable ground for the only kind of life we know, providing the sole sustenance of our minds and bodies, so does empirical truth constitute the foundation of higher truths. (If there is such a thing as higher truth.) It seems to me that Keats was wrong when he asked, rhetorically, "Do not all charms fly . . . at the mere touch of cold philosophy?" The word "philosophy" standing, in his day, for what we now call "physical science." But Keats was wrong, I say, because there is more charm in one "mere" fact, confirmed by test and observation, linked to other facts through coherent theory into a rational system, than in a whole brainful of fancy and fantasy. I see more poetry in a chunk of quartzite than in a make-believe wood nymph, more beauty in the revelations of a verifiable intellectual construction than in whole misty empires of obsolete mythology.

The moral I labor toward is that a landscape as splendid as that of the Colorado Plateau can best be understood and given human significance by poets who have their feet planted in concrete—concrete data—and by scientists whose heads and hearts have not lost the capacity for wonder. Any good poet, in our age at least, must begin with the scientific view of the world; and any scientist worth listening to must be something of a poet, must possess the ability to communicate to the rest of us his sense of love and wonder at what his work discovers.

The canyon country does not always inspire love. To many it appears barren, hostile, repellent—a fearsome land of rock and heat, sand dunes and quicksand, cactus, thornbush, scorpion, rattlesnake, and agoraphobic distances. To those who see our land in that manner, the best reply is, yes, you are right, it is a dangerous and terrible place. Enter at your own risk. Carry water. Avoid the noonday sun. Try to ignore the vultures. Pray frequently.

For a few others the canyon country is worth only what they can dig out of it and haul away—to the mills, to the power plants, to the bank.

For more and more of those who now live here, however, the great plateau and its canyon wilderness is a treasure best enjoyed through the body and spirit, *in situ* as the archeologists say, not through commercial plunder. It is a regional, national and international treasure too valuable to be sacrificed for temporary gain, too rare to be withheld from our children. For us the wilderness and human emptiness of this land is not a source of fear but the greatest of its attractions. We would guard and defend and save it as a place for all who wish to rediscover the nearly lost pleasures of adventure, adventure not only in the physical sense, but also mental, spiritual, moral, aesthetic and intellectual adventure. A place for the free.

Here you may yet find the elemental freedom to breathe deep of unpoisoned air, to experiment with solitude and stillness, to gaze through a hundred miles of untrammeled atmosphere, across redrock canyons, beyond blue mesas, toward the snow-covered peaks of the most distant mountains—to make the discovery of

5

the self in its proud sufficiency which is not isolation
but an irreplaceable part of the mystery of the whole.
Come on in. The earth, like the sun, like the air,
belongs to everyone—and to no one.

Edward Abbey

Plates

Plate 1

Plate 2

Plate 3

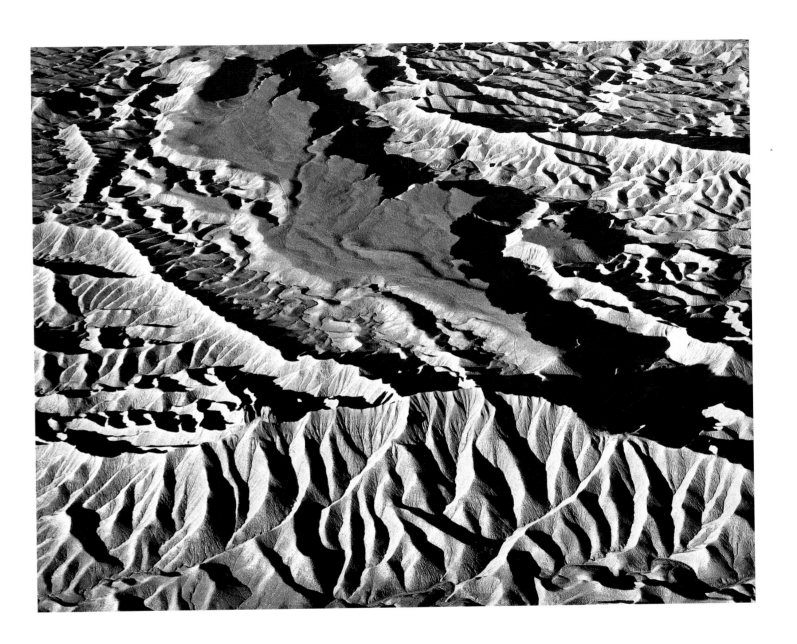

Plate 4

Plate 5

Plate 6

Plate 7

Plate 8

Plate 9

Plate 10

Plate 11

Plate 12

Plate 13

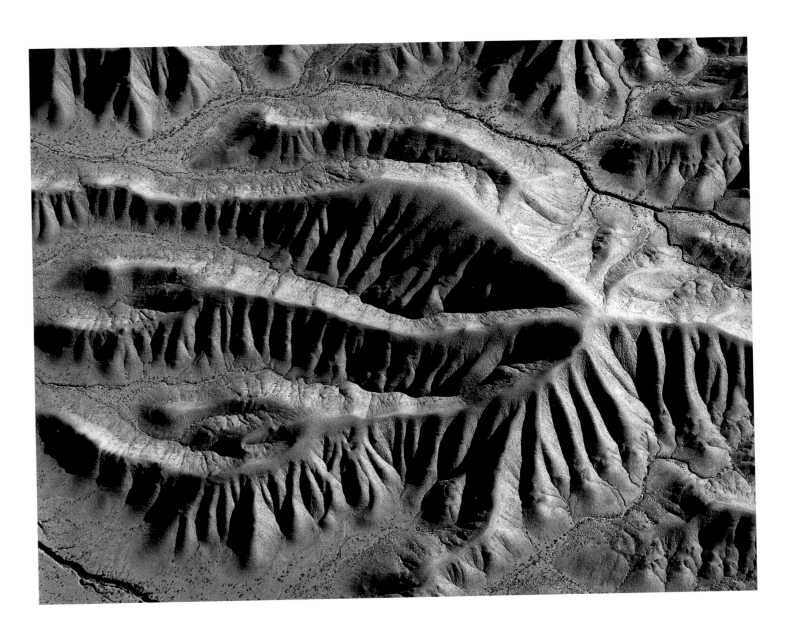

Plate 14

Plate 15

Plate 16

Plate 17

Plate 18

Plate 19

Plate 20

Plate 21

Plate 22

Plate 23

Plate 24

Plate 25

Plate 26

Plate 27

Plate 28

Plate 29

Plate 30

Plate 31

Plate 32

Plate 33

Plate 34

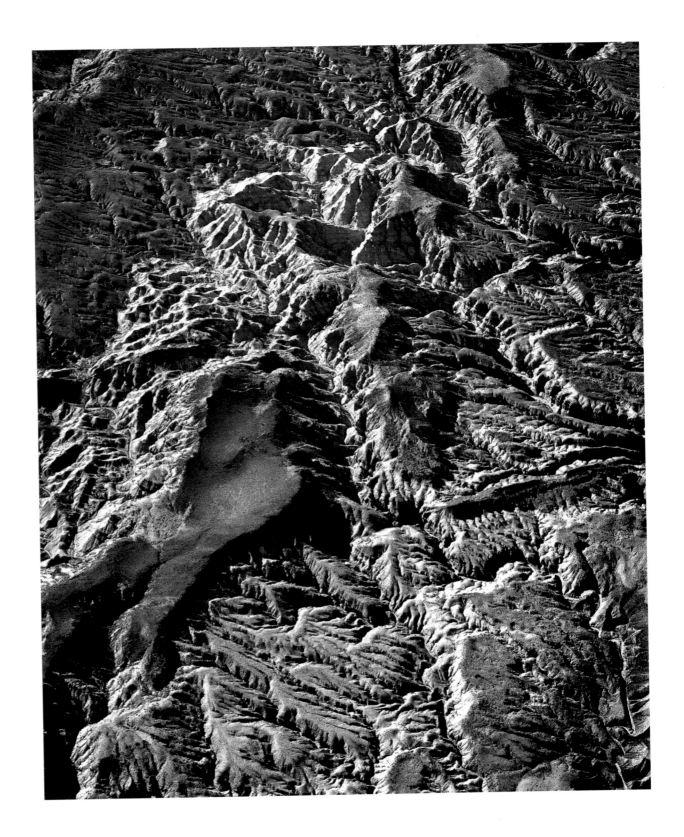

Plate 35

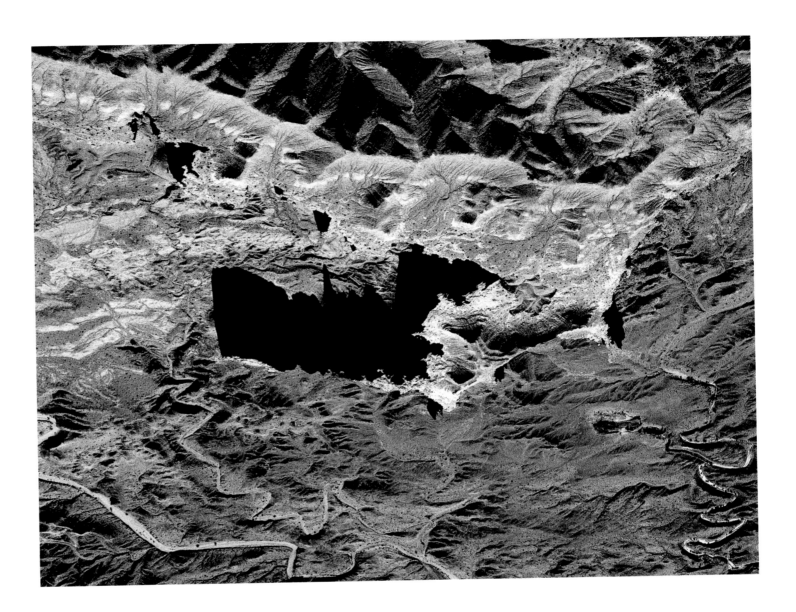

Plate 36

Plate 37

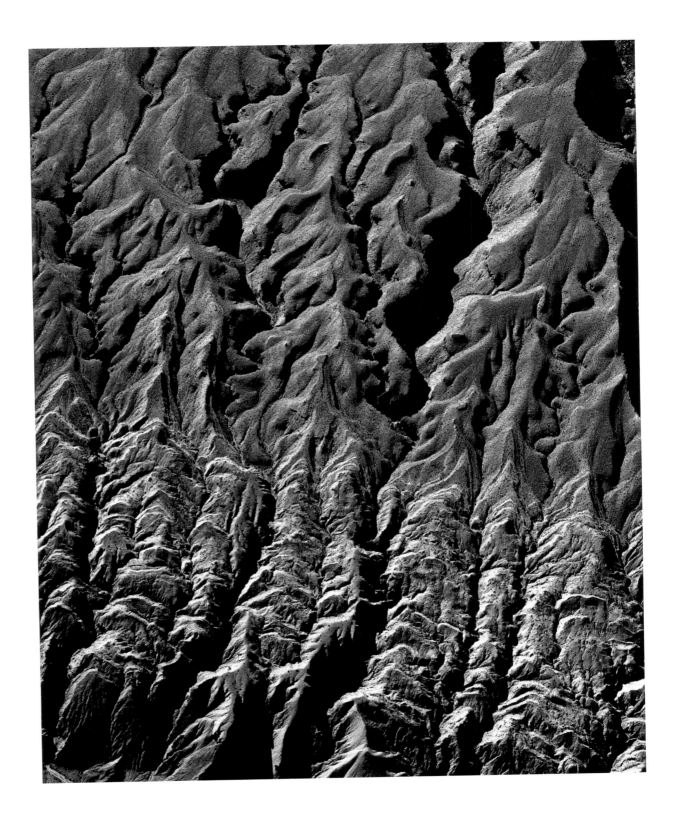

Plate 38

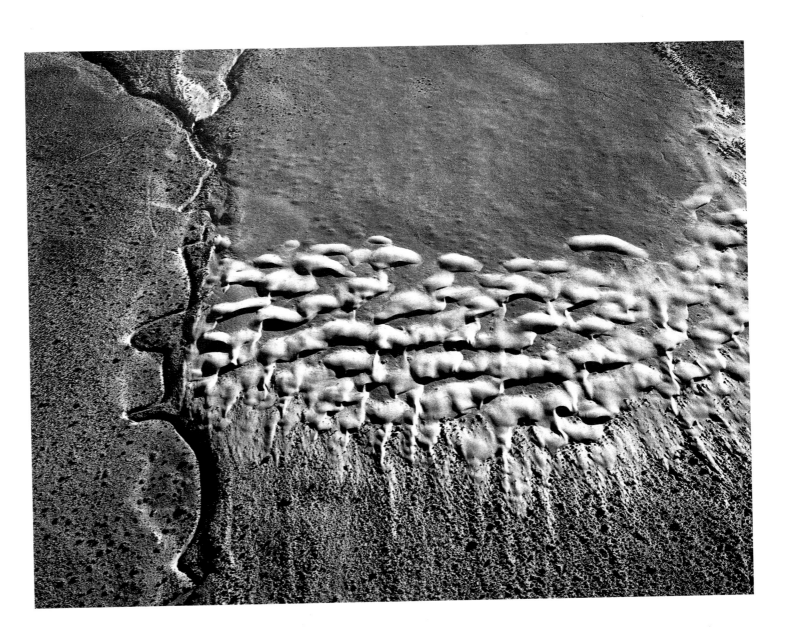

Plate 39

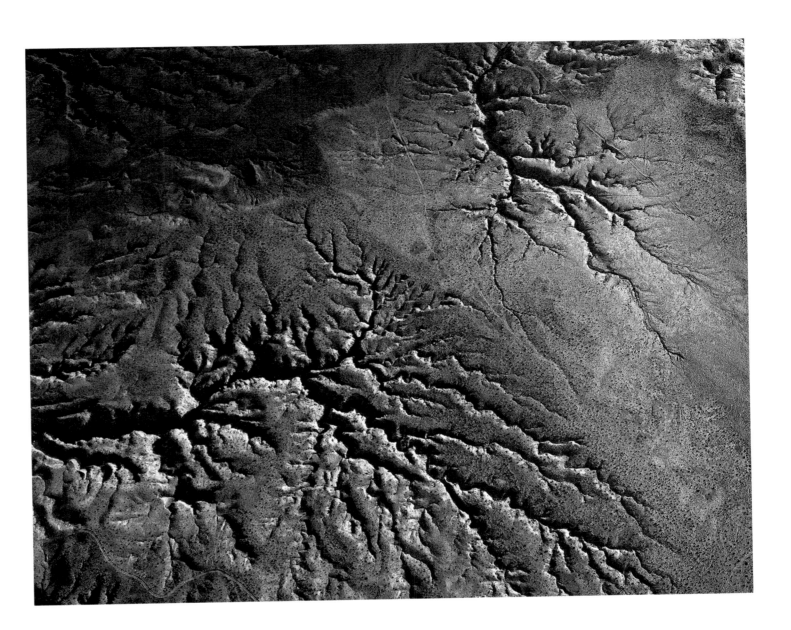

Plate 40

Plate 41

Plate 42

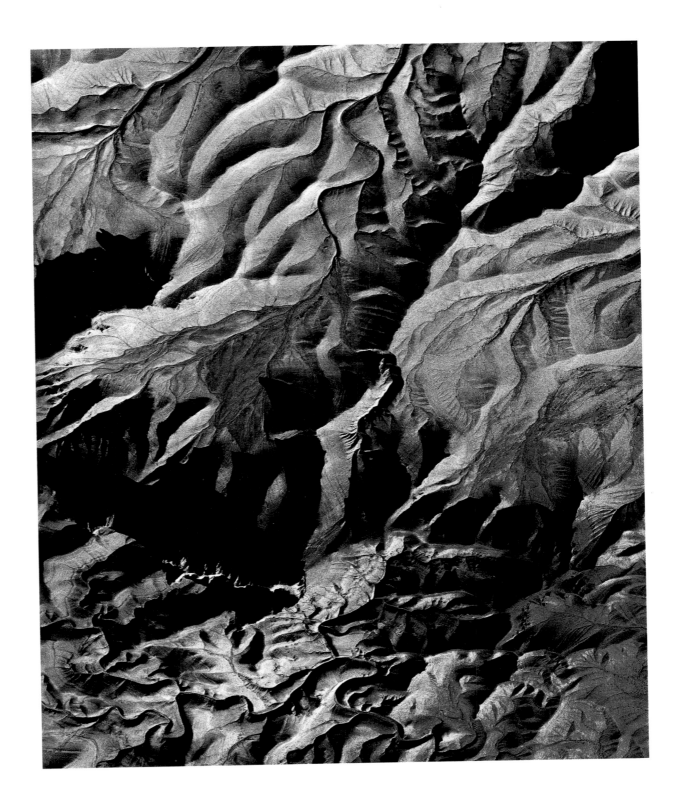

Afterword

These photographs were taken on the Colorado Plateau in the high desert of the American Southwest. Many were taken from the air, through the open window of a small airplane, as part of a wilderness documentation project in Utah.

Deeply etched by the Colorado River and its many tributaries, the plateau is defined by Precambrian faults half-a-billion years old. It is a microcosm of all that is extraordinary about the earth's crust. For me it is also a landscape of the mind and senses. Here, in the depths of solitude, I often see unexpected things and experience unexpected thoughts.

I created these images as a personal narrative of my experiences upon the Colorado Plateau. I do not expect any viewer's response to this work to mirror my own. In fact I will consider these photographs most successful if they elicit a variety of responses.

Deserts are landscapes of the past where we can see

things our distant ancestors saw and can wonder about the persistence of racial memory. My work in this particular desert began as an instinctive response to qualities of desert light and form that seemed to possess an intangible, mysterious significance at a particular instant.

Like dreams, photographs cannot be planned. I was well into my work before it occurred to me that I might be investigating something more tangible than momentary impression. I became aware of a communication between me and this desert skin and of a feeling that I was not choosing my subjects so much as they were choosing me. Too much solitude? Too much sun? Nevertheless, these feelings gave me a very personal sense that the earth's skin may be more a muse than we know.

Such thoughts accompanied a sense of eerie familiarity. I often felt I was looking at earth forms that are competent rough studies for the accoutrements of human civilization. The history of art is here, from figurative sculpture to abstract expressionism. Immense, silent cities of pyramids, ziggurats, temples, and cathedrals stand beside walls, arches, and domes, recording architectural history. Mathematics, from Euclid's geometries to networks and sets of a higher order, can also be discerned. Natural markings on stone suggest written language. Looking further, one sees a wheel, a gear, a knife blade. . . . Was our species given at birth a naturally formed blueprint for human invention? For human history? Have we spent the last ten thousand years (a relatively brief episode in our past) implementing this blueprint by creating the farms, towns, and other paraphernalia of civilization that so effectively insulate us from the landscape of our origins?

One morning, looking at proof sheets of aerial photographs, I noticed that some images took on a very different character when I inverted them, improbable yet believable. Concave became convex and vice versa throughout an entire image, totally transforming it. When I felt they were more expressive in the "upside down" position, I composed them that way. (Of course, there really is no upside down or rightside up when one is flying in a small airplane over the Colorado Plateau.) Many images suggested illustrations for works of science fiction, and I was reminded that writers of this genre often find inspiration in the desert. A late chapter in the blueprint? An early one?

Printing these negatives, I tried to interpret them in a manner consistent with my original reasons for exposing the film to light. I was unwilling to give up the texture of this tactile, sensuous, desert skin for the open whites favored by proponents of classical printing technique. Likewise, I sometimes found myself printing down blacks, eliminating shadow detail, in an attempt to recapture the sense of mysterious past that lingers on the great plateau. Some of the images that emerged in my developing tray were only remotely related to the brilliant silver-gelatin emulsion of the contemporary photograph. They seemed closer kin to dark images seen on old lithography stones, to dense, graphite drawings on yellowed parchment, or to the time-tempered cave paintings of Altamira and Lascaux. I tried to let them have their own life, wondering whether I was printing photographs or decoding messages from a paleolithic past.

After the American Civil War, a number of expeditionary groups used photography to document the western landscape. Intentionally or not, these surveys helped pave the way for the westward migration of European settlers. It is ironic that today, little more than a century later, parts of the West are being photographed to document the remnants of that once vast wilderness.

In the first half of the twentieth century, western landscape photography officially entered the world of art. This development was dominated by the work of Edward Weston, Ansel Adams, the f/64 group, and their followers. For these photographers, the landscape of the American West served as inspiration for works of powerful personal expression. Such images dominated western fine-art landscape photography until recently.

A current trend in landscape photography is to document ways in which the human race is altering the earth. This is important work, since we are changing the planet in ways that may eventually threaten our survival as a species. But I think we are not destroying the earth—only reducing our habitat. If it is the purpose of this "new" landscape photography to document change, I think it is successful. If its purpose is to instill a sense of respect for the earth, its success is marginal. If there is a way to alter our environmental practices through photography, it is to make images not only of what we are doing to the earth but also of what the earth has done for us.

Indigenous peoples have survived for thousands of years, sustained by the belief that they belong to the earth rather than the opposite. We of the self-designated post-industrial age would do well to adopt such a view. After all, it is we who are at the earth's mercy.

Thomas Miller

Acknowledgments

Many have influenced and contributed to this work. They are too numerous to list, but I wish to express heartfelt thanks to all. I am most grateful to my parents, Philip and Jessie Miller for all they have done. I also wish to express special appreciation to Carter Manny, Jr., and the Graham Foundation for professional and financial support; to Dale and Frandee Johnson for hours of flying time and good companionship; to Robertson Ward, Jr., Ezra Gordon, Philip Chen, Nancy Nesewich, Lenny Anderson, Rick Shorten, Greg Ware, Salauddin Khan, Howard Mason, Dana Spielmann, and Jane Kayl for years of professional support freely given; to Carole Ivy and Heath Silberfeld for editorial assistance; and to Susan Tixier and the staff of the Southern Utah Wilderness Alliance for reliable counsel concerning wilderness areas of the Colorado Plateau. I am especially indebted to my editor, Jeff Grathwohl, for his unfaltering commitment to this work, and to the University of Utah Press for publishing it.

Biography

Although he has been taking photographs since childhood, Thomas Miller was trained as an architect. In 1986 he left a professorship in Chicago to devote himself to photography. He now lives in Portland, Oregon, where he is an adjunct faculty member at the Pacific Northwest College of Art. His work has been published both regionally and nationally. Most recently, he was the primary contributing photographer for *Wilderness at the Edge* (1990), an edited volume introduced by the late Wallace Stegner. Mr. Miller's photographs have won major awards at the Oregon Biennial and from the Graham Foundation for Advanced Study in the Fine Arts in Chicago.